Fascinating Food Chains

Deciduous Forest Food Chains

By Julia Vogel

Illustrated by Hazel Adams

Content Consultant
Jacques Finlay, PhD
Assistant Professor
Department of Ecology,
Evolution, and Behavior
University of Minnesota

magic wagon

Printed in the United States of America, North Mankato, Minnesota.
042010
092010

 THIS BOOK CONTAINS AT LEAST 10% RECYCLED MATERIALS.

Text by Julia Vogel
Illustrations by Hazel Adams
Edited by Nadia Higgins
Interior layout and design by Nicole Brecke
Cover design by Kazuko Collins

Library of Congress Cataloging-in-Publication Data
Vogel, Julia.
  Deciduous forest food chains / by Julia Vogel ; illustrated by Hazel Adams.
    p. cm. — (Fascinating food chains)
  Includes index.
  ISBN 978-1-60270-792-4
  1. Forest ecology—Juvenile literature. 2. Food chains (Ecology)—Juvenile literature. I. Adams, Hazel, 1983- ill. II. Title.
  QH541.5.F6V64 2011
  577.3'—dc22
                        2009050437

Table of Contents

A Deciduous Forest Food Chain

A food chain tells us who eats what. It shows how living things need each other. Let's find out what's for dinner in the deciduous forest!

In one forest food chain, maple tree seeds come first. A white-footed mouse scurries over and gobbles them up. But the mouse can also be a meal. A long-tailed weasel eats the little furry animal. Then, high above, a great horned owl spots the weasel. It swoops down and attacks.

Seeds to mouse to weasel to owl. That's a simple food chain. But a gray squirrel also chomps on the maple tree seeds. Another food chain begins. It connects with other food chains, making a food web.

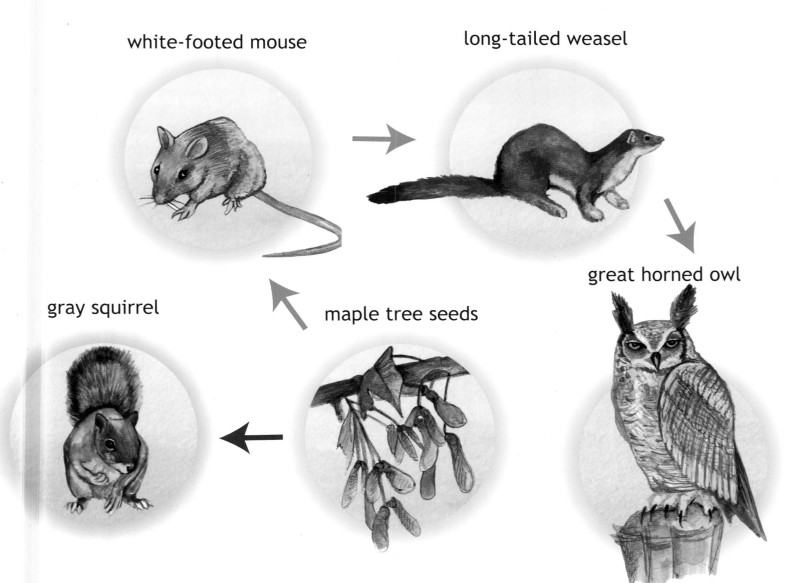

white-footed mouse

long-tailed weasel

great horned owl

gray squirrel

maple tree seeds

Food gives living things the energy and the nutrients they need to stay alive. The arrows show which way food's nutrients and energy move through this deciduous forest food chain.

Changing Forests

Deciduous forests change with the seasons. In summer, deciduous forests are warm and green. Animals find plenty to eat. But as autumn comes, the air grows cool. Flowers die. Yellow, red, and orange leaves drift down. In winter, snow blankets the ground. Yet owls, bears, and many other creatures live here all year long. Their amazing food chains help them survive.

Deciduous means "falling off." Much of the eastern United States is covered by deciduous forests. Canada, Russia, and Japan also have forests that lose their leaves each fall.

Plants Come First

Plants are the first link in the food chain. They need water and sunlight to make food. Rain and melted snow usually give them enough water. But how do plants get enough sunshine in the shady forest?

In early spring, bare trees let sunshine stream through. Ferns and flowers sprout quickly. Soon, tree leaves shade the forest floor. By now, however, the forest plants grow well in shade.

Many deciduous trees have flat, wide leaves that capture lots of sunlight. Their leaves are unlike pine needles and the leaves of other evergreen trees.

Herbivores Eat Plants

On a summer day, a white-footed mouse gobbles seeds from a maple tree. High above, millions of caterpillars munch on leaves. These animals are herbivores. They eat plants. The lush, green forest offers herbivores much to eat. They are the next food chain link.

Carnivores Eat Meat

A long-tailed weasel chases a white-footed mouse inside a hollow log. The weasel catches the mouse in its teeth. It feasts on its dinner. Nutrients and energy from the maple seeds the mouse ate end up inside the weasel.

Animals that eat other animals are carnivores. They are the next link in the food chain.

Weasels and other carnivores that hunt animals are called predators. The animals they hunt are called prey. Leafy forests can hide prey, but predators still find plenty to eat.

13

Top Carnivores Rule

The weasel lets down its guard. A great horned owl swoops down. The fierce bird grabs the furry weasel. She will share her catch with her young.

The owl is a top carnivore. It eats other meat eaters. Top carnivores rule the food chain. Usually, no other animals attack them.

Fall Changes

By late summer, the air is chilly, and colorful leaves fall. Many insects die. Such changes mean much less food in the winter. Some birds fly to warmer places. Other animals spend the winter in a deep sleep. A black bear may sleep for weeks in a hollow tree. On warmer winter days, it wakes up and searches for food.

In winter, salamanders burrow into the mud. Snakes tangle together under a pile of rocks. They do not need to eat again until spring.

17

The Snowy Winter

In winter, animals need extra food energy to stay warm. How do they find enough food?

Many animals change what they eat. Deer switch from green leaves to twigs and bark. Omnivores eat both plants and animals. A bear may eat frozen blackberries or a weasel it catches in the snow.

Decomposers Clean Up

A bear may eat most of a deer. Then decomposers, such as mushrooms, worms, and bacteria, take their turn on the leftovers. These tiny creatures also break down lots of dead plants, wood, and animal waste. As they do, they put nutrients back in the soil. This helps forest plants grow.

Decomposers can also be food for animals. Squirrels nibble mushrooms. Skunks dig worms from the soil.

Spring at Last

At last, the days grow long and warm. The forest becomes green again. Herbivores feast on the new leaves. Bees sip sweet nectar from flowers.

Meat eaters feast, too. The birds that flew away last fall return to eat insects. Bears search the woods for deer. Many predators are also on the hunt.

Spring is the wettest season in the forest. Shallow ponds appear, and frogs lay eggs there. Soon raccoons go to the ponds to enjoy tadpole breakfasts.

People and the Food Chain

American Indians have long found food in deciduous forests.
They collected sap from maple trees. They gathered nuts.
They picked blueberries, and they hunted deer.

Early white settlers also learned to hunt and gather from the forests.
For thousands of years, people have been part of deciduous forest food
chains.

But people can damage forests. They may cut down trees for wood or to make paper. They clear forests to make room for farms and cities.

Even if new trees are planted, the forest is never the same. Some plants do not grow back. If one link in a food chain disappears, other links that depend on it may vanish also.

Trees can live hundreds of years. Forests where the old trees have never been cut down are called old-growth forests.

You can help keep forests healthy. Recycle your papers at home and school. Help a nature center plant more trees. Most important, learn as much as you can about forests. Tell your friends how important and interesting deciduous forests are!

Some animals and plants in deciduous forests could die out. This weakens the food chain.

Food Chain Science

Scientists study forest food chains and food webs. They need to learn about all the ways plants and animals are connected. This helps them understand and protect important habitats.

The deciduous forests in the eastern United States are part-time homes to many kinds of songbirds. Warblers nest in these forests but spend the rest of the year in Central and South America. But shrinking forests everywhere are causing the birds to disappear. Smaller forests limit the space the warblers have to raise young and find food.

Scientists looked closer at the problem. In remaining forests, they counted fewer birds than in the past. The scientists discovered there were fewer plants for the birds to eat and nest in. What was happening to the plants?

Researchers found deer were eating the plants. They put up fences around some forest areas to keep the deer out. Many plants that the birds need grew back. The studies show that limiting deer populations can help protect songbirds. By studying how food webs interconnect, scientists learn how to protect animals and plants in forests and around the world.

Fun Facts

You can walk 2,175 miles (3,500 km) through forests in the eastern United States. Just follow the Appalachian Trail from Georgia to Maine.

The sweet-tasting seeds of beech trees once attracted billions of passenger pigeons. So many of the hungry birds would land on a tree that its branches would break.

Dead trees are as important as living trees to forest wildlife. Insects that chew up dead trees become food for termites, woodpeckers, skunks, and many other wild animals.

White-tailed deer are more common now than when settlers first arrived in North America. Few wolves and mountain lions are left to prey on deer, so their numbers are growing.

Tree seeds often sprout in the rotted remains of fallen logs. These dead trees are nurseries for baby trees. They are called nurse logs.

Blue jays help plant the forest. Each jay buries hundreds of tree seeds each fall to eat later. Any seed it doesn't find may sprout into a tree.

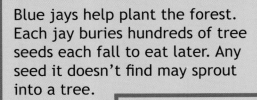

Words to Know

bacteria - tiny living things that help break down dead plants and animals. Bacteria can only be seen with a microscope.

carnivore - an animal that eats another animal.

decomposers - tiny living things that live on the dead remains of plants and animals as well as animal waste.

energy - power needed to work or live.

herbivore - an animal that eats plants.

nutrients - chemicals that plants and animals need to live.

omnivore - an animal that eats plants and animals.

top carnivore - a carnivore that is not preyed on by other carnivores.

On the Web

To learn more about deciduous forest food chains, visit ABDO Group online at **www.abdopublishing.com**. Web sites about deciduous forest food chains are featured on our Book Links page. These links are routinely monitored and updated to provide the most current information available.

Index